World's Best-Loved Poetry

Acknowledgments

E. E. CUMMINGS: "maggie and milly and molly and may." Copyright © 1956, 1984, 1991 by the Trustees for the E. E. Cummings Trust, from COMPLETE POEMS: 1904-1962 by E. E. Cummings, edited by George J. Firmage. Used by permission of Liveright Publishing Corporation.

EMILY DICKINSON: All poems except "I'm nobody! Who are you?" were originally published in POEMS by Emily Dickinson in 1890. "I'm nobody! Who are you?" was originally published in POEMS, SECOND SERIES in 1891.

ROBERT FROST: "Stopping by Woods on a Snowy Evening" and "The Road Not Taken" from THE POETRY OF ROBERT FROST edited by Edward Connery Lathem. Copyright 1923, © 1969 by Henry Holt and Company, copyright 1951 by Robert Frost. Reprinted by permission of Henry Holt and Company, LLC.

KAHLIL GIBRAN: "I am forever walking upon these shores" and "My house says to me, 'Do not leave me,'". From SAND AND FOAM by Kahlil Gibran, copyright © 1926 by Kahlil Gibran and renewed 1954 by Administrators C.T.A. of Kahlil Gibran Estate and Mary G. Gibran. Used by permission of Alfred A. Knopf, a division of Random House, Inc.

EDGAR A. GUEST: "On Quitting." Originally published in JUST FOLKS by Edgar A. Guest (Chicago: Reilly & Lee, 1917); "The Rough Little Rascal," "A Patriotic Wish," "Selfish," and "Failures" originally published in A HEAP O' LIVIN' by Edgar A. Guest (Chicago: Reilly & Lee, 1916).

ROBERT HAYDEN: "Those Winter Sundays." Copyright © 1966 by Robert Hayden, from ANGLE OF ASCENT: New and Selected Poems by Robert Hayden. Used by permission of Liveright Publishing Corporation.

(Acknowledgments are continued on page 128.)

ISBN 0-8167-7473-0

Printed in Canada.

10 9 8 7 6 5 4 3 2

Contents

Foreword

Poetry has been a part of the human experience for thousands of years. People around the world read and listen to poetry for many reasons. A favorite poem can make you feel happy or sad, or it can remind you of a special time in your life. Some people read poems because they love to listen to the rhythm the poet has created with words. Other people like to listen to poetry and to picture in their minds the images the poet writes about.

Whatever your reason for reading poetry, you'll find some of the best-loved poems ever written in this collection. From William Shakespeare's sonnets to Carl Sandburg's stunning word pictures, you'll find poems about topics such as love, nature, people, places, and animals. Choose a topic and read all the poems in that section, or find a poem that fits your mood. Share a favorite poem with a friend, and let the special people in your life know how you feel. You'll find something new and different every time you open this book. As John Keats said, "A thing of beauty is a joy forever," and these timeless poems will continue to delight readers for generations to come.

Nature

Daybreak

Daybreak comes first
   in thin splinters shimmering.
Neither is the day here
   nor is the night gone.
Night is getting ready to go
And Day whispers, "Soon now, soon."

CARL SANDBURG

Pippa's Song

The year's at the spring
And the day's at the morn;
Morning's at seven;
The hillside's dew-pearled;
The lark's on the wing;
The snail's on the thorn:
God's in his heaven—
All's right with the world!

ROBERT BROWNING

April Rain Song

Let the rain kiss you.
Let the rain beat upon your head with silver liquid drops.
Let the rain sing you a lullaby.

The rain makes still pools on the sidewalk.
The rain makes running pools in the gutter.
The rain plays a little sleep-song on our roof at night—

And I love the rain.

LANGSTON HUGHES

An April Day

On such a day as this I think,
      On such a day as this,
When earth and sky and nature's whole
      Are clad in April's bliss;
And balmy zephyrs gently waft
      Upon your cheek a kiss;
Sufficient is it just to live
      On such a day as this.

JOSEPH SEAMON COTTER, JR.

The Daffodils

I wander'd lonely as a cloud
That floats on high o'er vales and hills,
When all at once I saw a crowd,
A host of golden daffodils,
Beside the lake, beneath the trees
Fluttering and dancing in the breeze.

Continuous as the stars that shine
And twinkle on the milky way,
They stretch'd in never-ending line
Along the margin of a bay:
Ten thousand saw I at a glance
Tossing their heads in sprightly dance.

The waves beside them danced, but they
Out-did the sparkling waves in glee:—
A Poet could not but be gay
In such a jocund company!
I gazed—and gazed—but little thought
What wealth the show to me had brought;

For oft, when on my couch I lie
In vacant or in pensive mood,
They flash upon that inward eye
Which is the bliss of solitude;
And then my head with pleasure fills,
And dances with the daffodils.

WILLIAM WORDSWORTH

Fog

The fog comes
on little cat feet.

It sits looking
over harbor and city
on silent haunches
and then moves on.

CARL SANDBURG

from *I Like It When It's Mizzly*

I like it when it's mizzly
and just a little drizzly
so everything looks far away
and make-believe and frizzly.

AILEEN FISHER

My heart leaps up when I behold

My heart leaps up when I behold
   A rainbow in the sky:
So was it when my life began,
   So is it now I am a man,
So be it when I shall grow old
     Or let me die!
The child is father of the man:
And I could wish my days to be
Bound each to each by natural piety.

WILLIAM WORDSWORTH

Summer Shower

A drop fell on the apple-tree,
Another on the roof;
A half a dozen kissed the eaves,
And made the gables laugh.

A few went out to help the brook,
That went to help the sea.
Myself conjectured, Were they pearls,
What necklaces could be!

The dust replaced in hoisted roads,
The birds jocoser sung;
The sunshine threw his hat away,
The orchards spangles hung.

The breezes brought dejected lutes,
And bathed them in the glee;
The East put out a single flag,
And signed the fête away.

EMILY DICKINSON

I am forever walking upon these shores,

I am forever walking upon these shores,
Betwixt the sand and the foam,
The high tide will erase my foot-prints,
And the wind will blow away the foam.
But the sea and the shore will remain
Forever.

KAHLIL GIBRAN

Autumn

The morns are meeker than they were,
The nuts are getting brown;
The berry's cheek is plumper,
The rose is out of town.

The maple wears a gayer scarf,
The field a scarlet gown.
Lest I should be old-fashioned,
I'll put a trinket on.

EMILY DICKINSON

The Sun Has Set

The sun has set, and the long grass now
    Waves dreamily in the evening wind;
And the wild bird has flown from that old gray stone
    In some warm nook a couch to find.

In all the lonely landscape round
    I see no light and hear no sound,
Except the wind that far away
    Come sighing o'er the healthy sea.

EMILY BRONTË

Winter Trees

All the complicated details
of the attiring and
the disattiring are completed!
A liquid moon
moves gently among
the long branches.
Thus having prepared their buds
against a sure winter
the wise trees
stand sleeping in the cold.

WILLIAM CARLOS WILLIAMS

Over the wintry

Over the wintry
forest, winds howl in a rage
with no leaves to blow.

SOSEKI

Snow-Flakes

Out of the bosom of the Air
　　Out of the cloud-folds of her garments shaken,
Over the woodlands brown and bare,
　　Over the harvest-fields forsaken,
　　　Silent, and soft, and slow
　　　Descends the snow.

Even as our cloudy fancies take
　　Suddenly shape in some divine expression,
Even as the troubled heart doth make
　　In the white countenance confession
　　　The troubled sky reveals
　　　The grief it feels.

This is the poem of the air,
　　Slowly in silent syllables recorded;
This is the secret of despair,
　　Long in its cloudy bosom hoarded,
　　　Now whispered and revealed
　　　To wood and field.

HENRY WADSWORTH LONGFELLOW

December

The lakes of ice gleam bluer than the lakes
Of water 'neath the summer sunshine gleamed:
Far fairer than when placidly it streamed,
The brook its frozen architecture makes,
And under bridges white its swift way takes.
Snow comes and goes as messenger who dreamed
Might linger on the road; or one who deemed
His message hostile gently for their sakes
Who listened might reveal it by degrees.
We gird against the cold of winter wind
Our loins now with mighty bands of sleep,
In longest, darkest nights take rest and ease,
And every shortening day, as shadows creep
O'er the brief noontide, fresh surprises find.

HELEN HUNT JACKSON

The Stars

They wait all day unseen by us, unfelt;
Patient they bide behind the day's full glare;
And we, who watched the dawn when they were there,
Thought we had seen them in the daylight melt,
While the slow sun upon the earth-line knelt.
Because the teeming sky seemed void and bare,
When we explored it through the dazzled air,
We had no thought that there all day they dwelt.
Yet were they over us, alive and true,
In the vast shades far up above the blue,—
The brooding shades beyond our daylight ken,—
Serene and patient in their conscious light,
Ready to sparkle for our joy again,—
The eternal jewels of the short-lived night.

MARY MAPES DODGE

Places

from America the Beautiful

O beautiful for spacious skies,
　For amber waves of grain,
For purple mountain majesties
　Above the fruited plain!
　　America! America!
　God shed his grace on thee
And crown thy good with brotherhood
　From sea to shining sea!

O beautiful for pilgrim feet,
　Whose stern, impassioned stress
A thoroughfare for freedom beat
　Across the wilderness!
　　America! America!
　God mend thine every flaw,
Confirm thy soul in self-control,
　Thy liberty in law!

O beautiful for heroes proved
　In liberating strife.
Who more than self the country loved,
　And mercy more than life!
　　America! America!
　May God thy gold refine,
Till all success be nobleness,
　And every gain divine!

O beautiful for patriot dream
   That sees beyond the years
Thine alabaster cities gleam
   Undimmed by human tears!
    America! America!
   God shed his grace on thee
And crown thy good with brotherhood
   From sea to shining sea!

KATHARINE LEE BATES

The Road Not Taken

Two roads diverged in a yellow wood
And sorry I could not travel both
And be one traveler, long I stood
And looked down one as far as I could
To where it bent in the undergrowth;

Then took the other, as just as fair,
And having perhaps the better claim,
Because it was grassy and wanted wear;
Though as for that the passing there
Had worn them really about the same,

And both that morning equally lay
In leaves no step had trodden black.
Oh, I kept the first for another day!
Yet knowing how way leads on to way,
I doubted if I should ever come back.

I shall be telling this with a sigh
Somewhere ages and ages hence:
Two roads diverged in a wood, and I—
I took the one less traveled by,
And that has made all the difference.

ROBERT FROST

City

In the morning the city
Spreads its wings
Making a song
In stone that sings.

In the evening the city
Goes to bed
Hanging lights
About its head.

LANGSTON HUGHES

Composed upon Westminster Bridge

Earth has not anything to show more fair:
Dull would he be of soul who could pass by
A sight so touching in its majesty:
This city now doth, like a garment, wear
The beauty of the morning; silent, bare,
Ships, towers, domes, theatres, and temples lie
Open unto the fields, and to the sky;
All bright and glittering in the smokeless air.
Never did sun more beautifully steep
In his first splendour, valley, rock, or hill;
Ne'er saw I, never felt, a calm so deep!
The river glideth at his own sweet will:
Dear God! the very houses seem asleep;
And all that mighty heart is lying still!

WILLIAM WORDSWORTH

I Love to Be Warm by the Red Fireside

I love to be warm by the red fireside,
I love to be wet with rain:
I love to be welcome at lamplit doors,
And leave the doors again.

ROBERT LOUIS STEVENSON

Stopping by Woods on a Snowy Evening

Whose woods these are I think I know.
His house is in the village though;
He will not see me stopping here
To watch his woods fill up with snow.

My little horse must think it queer
To stop without a farmhouse near
Between the woods and frozen lake
The darkest evening of the year.

He gives his harness bells a shake
To ask if there is some mistake.
The only other sound's the sweep
Of easy wind and downy flake.

The woods are lovely, dark and deep,
But I have promises to keep,
And miles to go before I sleep,
And miles to go before I sleep.

ROBERT FROST

The House on the Hill

They are all gone away,
    The house is shut and still,
There is nothing more to say.

Through broken walls and gray
    The winds blow bleak and shrill:
They are all gone away.

Nor is there one today
    To speak them good or ill:
There is nothing more to say.

Why is it then we stray
    Around the sunken sill?
They are all gone away.

And our poor fancy-play
    For them is wasted skill:
There is nothing more to say.

There is ruin and decay
    In the House on the Hill
They are all gone away,
There is nothing more to say.

EDWIN ARLINGTON ROBINSON

Animals

—

The Eagle

He clasps the crag with crooked hands;
Close to the sun in lonely lands,
Ring'd with the azure world, he stands.

The wrinkled sea beneath him crawls;
He watches from his mountain walls,
And like a thunderbolt he falls.

ALFRED, LORD TENNYSON

Winter downpour—

Winter downpour—
even the monkey
needs a raincoat.

BASHO

Jabberwocky

'Twas brillig, and the slithy toves
Did gyre and gimble in the wabe:
All mimsy were the borogoves,
And the mome raths outgrabe.

"Beware the Jabberwock, my son!
The jaws that bite, the claws that catch!
Beware the Jubjub bird, and shun
The frumious Bandersnatch!"

He took his vorpal sword in hand:
Long time the manxome foe he sought—
So rested he by the Tumtum tree,
And stood a while in thought.

And, as in uffish thought he stood,
The Jabberwock, with eyes of flame,
Came whiffling through the tulgey wood,
And burbled as it came!

One two! One two! And through and through
The vorpal blade went snicker-snack!
He left it dead, and with its head
He went galumphing back.

"And hast thou slain the Jabberwock?
Come to my arms, my beamish boy!
Oh frabjous day! Callooh! Callay!"
He chortled in his joy.

'Twas brillig, and the slithy toves
Did gyre and gimble in the wabe:
All mimsy were the borogoves,
And the mome raths outgrabe.

LEWIS CARROLL

The Scorpion

The Scorpion is as black as soot,
    He dearly loves to bite;
He is a most unpleasant brute
    To find in bed at night.

HILAIRE BELLOC

The Purple Cow

I never saw a Purple Cow;
  I never hope to See One;
But I can Tell you, Anyhow,
  I'd rather See than Be One.

GELETT BURGESS

The Goat Paths

The crooked paths go every way
Upon the hill—they wind about
Through the heather in and out
Of the quiet sunniness.
And there the goats, day after day,
Stray in sunny quietness,
Cropping here and cropping there,
As they pause and turn and pass,
Now a bit of heather spray,
Now a mouthful of the grass.

In the deeper sunniness,
In the place where nothing stirs,
Quietly in quietness,
In the quiet of the furze,
For a time they come and lie
Staring on the roving sky.

If you approach they run away,
They leap and stare, away they bound,
With a sudden angry sound,
To the sunny quietude;
Crouching down where nothing stirs
In the silence of the furze,
Crouching down again to brood
In the sunny solitude.

If I were as wise as they,
I would stray apart and brood,
I would beat a hidden way
Through the quiet heather spray
To a sunny solitude;

And should you come I'd run away,
I would make an angry sound,
I would stare and turn and bound
To the deeper quietude,
To the place where nothing stirs
In the silence of the furze.

In that airy quietness
I would think as long as they;
Through the quiet sunniness
I would stray away to brood
By a hidden, beaten way
In the sunny solitude,

I would think until I found
Something I can never find,
Something lying on the ground,
In the bottom of my mind.

JAMES STEPHENS

The Chimpanzee

Children, behold the Chimpanzee:
He sits on the ancestral tree
From which we sprang in ages gone.
I'm glad we sprang: had we held on,
We might, for aught that I can say,
Be horrid Chimpanzees to-day.

OLIVER HERFORD

How doth the little crocodile

How doth the little crocodile
    Improve his shining tail,
And pour the waters of the Nile
    On every golden scale!

How cheerfully he seems to grin
    How neatly spreads his claws,
And welcomes little fishes in,
    With gently smiling jaws!

LEWIS CARROLL

To the Oriole

Lightly swinging, sweetly singing,
　In the budding trees;
Rapturous song is borne along
　On the scented breeze.

Golden throated, joyous noted,
　In the bright spring days;
Happy creature! What a teacher
　Of the art of praise!

With thy trilling thou art filling
　All the balmy air;
Thine is pleasure without measure,
　Song is everywhere.

Cease your singing, cease your swinging,
　Fly unto your nest.
Shades are falling, night is calling
　Nature to its rest.

HERBERT SALISBURY HOPKINS

The Parrot and the Carrot

The Parrot and the Carrot we may easily confound,
They're very much alike in looks and similar in sound,
We recognize the Parrot by his clear articulation,
For Carrots are unable to engage in conversation.

ROBERT WILLIAMS WOOD

Early News

The sparrow told it to the robin,
The robin told it to the wren,
Who passed it on, with sweet remark,
To thrush, and bobolink, and lark,
The news that dawn had come again.

ANNA M. PRATT

Three little birds in a row

Three little birds in a row
Sat musing.
A man passed near that place.
Then did the little birds nudge each other.

They said, "He thinks he can sing."
They threw back their heads to laugh.
With quaint countenances
They regarded him.
They were very curious,
Those three little birds in a row.

STEPHEN CRANE

The Cat-bird and the Cat-nip

The Cat-bird's call resembles that,
Emitted by the Pussy Cat,
While Cat-nip, growing by the wall,
Is never known to caterwaul:
It's odor though attracts the Kits,
And throws them in Catniption fits.

ROBERT WILLIAMS WOOD

Flying Fish

Out where the sky and the sky-blue sea
  Merge in a mist of sheen,
There started a vision of silver things,
A leap and a quiver, a flash of wings
  The sky and the sea between.

Is it of birds from the blue above,
  Or fish from the depths that be?
    Or is it the ghosts
    In silver hosts
Of birds that were drowned at sea?

MARY MCNEIL FENOLLOSA

Love &

Friendship

To me, fair friend, you never can be old,

To me, fair friend, you never can be old,
For as you were when first your eye I eyed,
Such seems your beauty still. Three winters cold
Have from the forests shook three summers' pride,
Three beauteous springs to yellow autumn turn'd
In process of the seasons have I seen,
Three April perfumes in three hot Junes burn'd,
Since first I saw you fresh, which yet are green.
Ah! yet doth beauty, like a dial-hand,
Steal from his figure and no pace perceived;
So your sweet hue, which methinks still doth stand,
Hath motion and mine eye may be deceived:
    For fear of which, hear this, thou age unbred;
    Ere you were born was beauty's summer dead.

WILLIAM SHAKESPEARE

How do I love thee? Let me count the ways.

How do I love thee? Let me count the ways.
I love thee to the depth and breadth and height
My soul can reach, when feeling out of sight
For the ends of Being and ideal Grace.
I love thee to the level of everyday's
Most quiet need, by sun and candle-light.
I love thee freely, as men strive for Right;
I love thee purely, as they turn from Praise.
I love thee with the passion put to use
In my old griefs, and with my childhood's faith.
I love thee with a love I seemed to lose
With my lost saints,—I love thee with the breath,
Smiles, tears, of all my life!—and, if God choose,
I shall but love thee better after death.

ELIZABETH BARRETT BROWNING

Winds of May, that dance on the sea,

Winds of May, that dance on the sea,
Dancing a ring-around in glee
From furrow to furrow, while overhead
The foam flies up to be garlanded,
In silvery arches spanning the air,
Saw you my true love anywhere?
     Welladay! Welladay!
     For the winds of May!
Love is unhappy when love is away!

JAMES JOYCE

A Red, Red Rose

Oh my love's like a red, red rose
    That's newly sprung in June;
Oh my love's like the melody
    That's sweetly played in tune.

As fair art thou, my bonnie lass,
    So deep in love am I;
And I will love thee still, my dear,
    Till a' the seas gang dry.

Till a' the seas gang dry, my dear,
    And the rocks melt wi' the sun:
And I will love thee still, my dear,
    While the sands o' life shall run.

And fare thee weel, my only love!
    And fare thee weel, a while!
And I will come again, my love,
    Tho' it were ten thousand mile!

ROBERT BURNS

To My Dear and Loving Husband

If ever two were one, then surely we.
If ever man were loved by wife, then thee;
If ever wife was happy in a man,
Compare with me, ye women, if you can.
I prize thy love more than whole mines of gold,
Or all the riches that the East doth hold.
My love is such that rivers cannot quench,
Nor aught but love from thee give recompense.
Thy love is such I can no way repay,
The heavens reward thee manifold, I pray.
Then while we live, in love let's so perséver
That when we live no more, we may live ever.

ANNE BRADSTREET

Shall I compare thee to a summer's day?

Shall I compare thee to a summer's day?
Thou art more lovely and more temperate.
Rough winds do shake the darling buds of May,
And summer's lease hath all too short a date.
Sometime too hot the eye of heaven shines,
And often is his gold complexion dimmed;
And every fair from fair sometime declines,
By chance, or nature's changing course, untrimmed;
But thy eternal summer shall not fade,
Nor lose possession of that fair thou owest,
Nor shall death brag thou wanderest in his shade,
When in eternal lines to time thou growest.
   So long as men can breathe or eyes can see,
   So long lives this, and this gives life to thee.

WILLIAM SHAKESPEARE

The Poet pleads with his Friend for old Friend.

Though you are in your shining days,
Voices among the crowd
And new friends busy with your praise,
Be not unkind or proud,
But think about old friends the most:
Time's bitter flood will rise,
Your beauty perish and be lost
For all eyes but these eyes.

WILLIAM BUTLER YEATS

The Passionate Shepherd to His Love

Come live with me and be my love,
And we will all the pleasures prove
That valleys, groves, hills, and fields,
Woods, or steepy mountain yields.

And we will sit upon the rocks,
Seeing the shepherds feed their flocks,
By shallow rivers, to whose falls
Melodious birds sing madrigals.

And I will make thee beds of roses
And a thousand fragrant posies,
A cap of flowers, and a kirtle
Embroidered all with leaves of myrtle;

A gown made of the finest wool,
Which from our pretty lambs we pull;
Fair linèd slippers for the cold,
With buckles of the purest gold;

A belt of straw and ivy buds
With coral clasps and amber studs:
And if these pleasures may thee move,
Come live with me and be my love.

The shepherd swains shall dance and sing
For thy delight each May morning:
If these delights thy mind may move,
Then live with me and be my love.

CHRISTOPHER MARLOWE

To Helen

Helen, thy beauty is to me
    Like those Nicean barks of yore,
That gently, o'er a perfumed sea,
    The weary, way-worn wanderer bore
    To his own native shore.

On desperate seas long wont to roam,
    Thy hyacinth hair, thy classic face,
Thy Naiad airs have brought me home
    To the glory that was Greece,
And the grandeur that was Rome.

Lo! in yon brilliant window-niche
    How statue-like I see thee stand,
    The agate lamp within thy hand!
Ah, Psyche, from the regions which
    Are Holy-Land!

EDGAR ALLAN POE

When to the sessions of sweet silent thought

When to the sessions of sweet silent thought
I summon up remembrance of things past,
I sigh the lack of many a thing I sought,
And with old woes new wail my dear time's waste.
Then can I drown an eye, unused to flow,
For precious friends hid in death's dateless night,
And weep afresh love's long since canceled woe,
And moan the expense of many a vanished sight;
Then can I grieve at grievances foregone,
And heavily from woe to woe tell o'er
The sad account of fore-bemoanèd moan,
Which I new pay as if not paid before.
   But if the while I think on thee, dear friend,
   All losses are restored and sorrows end.

WILLIAM SHAKESPEARE

First time he kissed me, he but only kissed

First time he kissed me, he but only kissed
The fingers of this hand wherewith I write;
And ever since, it grew more clean and white,
Slow to world-greetings, quick with its "Oh, list,"
When the angels speak. A ring of amethyst
I could not wear here, plainer to my sight,
Than that first kiss. The second passed in height
The first, and sought the forehead, and half missed,
Half falling on the hair. O beyond meed!
That was the chrism of love, which love's own crown,
With sanctifying sweetness, did precede.
The third upon my lips was folded down
In perfect, purple state; since when, indeed,
I have been proud and said, "My love, my own."

ELIZABETH BARRETT BROWNING

When You Are Old

When you are old and gray and full of sleep,
And nodding by the fire, take down this book,
And slowly read, and dream of the soft look
Your eyes had once, and of their shadows deep;

How many loved your moments of glad grace,
And loved your beauty with love false or true,
But one man loved the pilgrim soul in you,
And loved the sorrows of your changing face;

And bending down beside the glowing bars,
Murmur, a little sadly, how love fled
And paced among the mountains overhead
And hid his face among a crowd of stars.

WILLIAM BUTLER YEATS

If I But Knew

If I but knew what the tree-tops say,
Whispering secrets night and day,
I'd make a song, my love, for you,
If I but knew—if I but knew.

If I but knew how the lilies brew
Nectar rare from a drop of dew,
A crystal glass I'd fill for you,
If I but knew—if I but knew.

Love, if I knew but one tender word,
Sweet as the note of a wooing bird,
I'd tell my ardent love to you,
If I but knew—if I but knew.

AMY E. LEIGH

We Were Boys Together

We were boys together,
   And never can forget
The school-house near the heather,
   In childhood where we met;
The humble home to memory dear,
   Its sorrows and its joys;
Where woke the transient smile or tear,
   When you and I were boys.

We were youths together,
   And castles built in air,
Your heart was like a feather,
   And mine weighed down with care;
To you came wealth with manhood's prime,
   To me it brought alloys—
Foreshadowed in the primrose time,
   When you and I were boys.

We're old men together:
   The friends we loved of yore,
With leaves of autumn weather,
   Are gone forevermore.
How blest to age the impulse given,
   The hope time ne'er destroys,
Which led our thoughts from earth to heaven
   When you and I were boys!

GEORGE POPE MORRIS

Outwitted

He drew a circle that shut me out—
    Heretic, a rebel, a thing to flout.
But Love and I had the wit to win:
    We drew a circle that took him in!

EDWIN MARKHAM

People

I'm nobody! Who are you?

I'm nobody! Who are you?
Are you nobody, too?
Then there's a pair of us—don't tell!
They'd banish us, you know.

How dreary to be somebody!
How public, like a frog
To tell your name the livelong day
To an admiring bog!

EMILY DICKINSON

I Hear America Singing

I hear America singing, the varied carols I hear,
Those of mechanics, each one singing his as it should be
   blithe and strong,
The carpenter singing his as he measures his plank or beam,
The mason singing his as he makes ready for work,
   or leaves off work,
The boatman singing what belongs to him in his boat,
   the deckhand singing on the steamboat deck,
The shoemaker singing as he sits on his bench, the hatter
   singing as he stands,
The wood-cutter's song, the ploughboy's on his way in the
   morning, or at noon intermission or at sundown,
The delicious singing of the mother, or of the young wife
   at work, or of the girl sewing or washing,
Each singing what belongs to him or her and to none else,
The day what belongs to the day—at night the party of
   young fellows, robust, friendly,
Singing with open mouths their strong melodious songs.

WALT WHITMAN

Lullaby of the Iroquois

Little brown baby-bird, lapped in your nest,
Wrapped in your nest,
Strapped in your nest,
Your straight little cradle-board rocks you to rest;
Its hands are your nest;
Its bands are your nest;
It swings from the down-bending branch of the oak;
You watch the camp flame, and the curling gray smoke;
But, oh, for your pretty black eyes sleep is best,—
Little brown baby of mine, go to rest.

Little brown baby-bird swinging to sleep,
Winging to sleep,
Singing to sleep,
Your wonder-black eyes that so wide open keep,
Shielding their sleep,
Unyielding to sleep,
The heron is homing, the plover is still,
The night-owl calls from his haunt on the hill,
Afar the fox barks, afar the stars peep,—
Little brown baby of mine, go to sleep.

E. Pauline Johnson (Tekahionwake)

from *Song of Myself*

am the mash'd fireman with breast-bone broken,
'umbling walls buried me in their debris,
Ieat and smoke I inspired, I heard the yelling shouts
  of my comrades,
heard the distant click of their picks and shovels,
'hey have clear'd the beams away, they tenderly lift me forth.

lie in the night air in my red shirt, the pervading hush is
  for my sake,
'ainless after all I lie exhausted but not so unhappy,
Vhite and beautiful are the faces around me, the heads are
  bared of their fire-caps,
'he kneeling crowd fades with the light of the torches.

WALT WHITMAN

On Quitting

How much grit do you think you've got?
Can you quit a thing that you like a lot?
You may talk of pluck; it's an easy word,
And where'er you go it is often heard;
But can you tell to a jot or a guess
Just how much courage you now possess?
You may stand to trouble and keep your grin,
But have you tackled self-discipline?
Have you ever issued commands to you
To quit the things that you like to do,
And then, when tempted and sorely swayed,
Those rigid orders have you obeyed?

Don't boast of your grit till you've tried it out,
Nor prate to men of your courage stout,
For it's easy enough to retain a grin
In the face of a fight there's a chance to win,
But the sort of grit that is good to own
Is the stuff you need when you're all alone.
How much grit do you think you've got?
Can you turn from joys that you like a lot?
Have you ever tested yourself to know
How far with yourself your will can go?
If you want to know if you have grit,
Just pick out a joy that you like, and quit.

It's bully sport and it's open fight;
It will keep you busy both day and night;
For the toughest kind of a game you'll find
Is to make your body obey your mind.
And you never will know what is meant by grit
Unless there's something you've tried to quit.

EDGAR A. GUEST

Brotherhood

The crest and crowning of all good,
Life's final star, is brotherhood;
For it will bring again to Earth
Her long-lost Poesy and Mirth;
Will send new light on every face,
A kingly power upon the race.
And till it come, we men are slaves,
And travel downward to the dust of graves.
Come, clear the way, then, clear the way;
Blind creeds and kings have had their day;
Break the dead branches from the path;
Our Hope is in the aftermath—
Our hope is in heroic men
Star-led to build the world again.
Make way for brotherhood—make way for Man!

EDWIN MARKHAM

Poet

To clothe the fiery thought
In simple words succeeds,
For still the craft of genius is
To mask a king in weeds.

RALPH WALDO EMERSON

from *Song of Myself*

I understand the large hearts of heroes,
The courage of present times and all times,
How the skipper saw the crowded and rudderless wreck of the
    steam-ship, and Death chasing it up and down the storm,
How he knuckled tight and gave not back an inch, and was
    faithful of days and faithful of nights,
And chalk'd in large letters on a board, Be of good cheer, we
    will not desert you;
How he follow'd with them and tack'd with them three days
    and would not give it up,
How he saved the drifting company at last,
How the lank loose-gown'd women look'd when boated from
    the side of their prepared graves,
How the silent old-faced infants and the lifted sick, and the
    sharp-lipp'd unshaved men;
All this I swallow, it tastes good, I like it well, it becomes mine,
I am the man, I suffer'd, I was there.

WALT WHITMAN

There was an Old Man with a beard,

There was an Old Man with a beard,
Who said "It is just as I feared!—
Two Owls and a Hen,
Four Larks and a Wren,
Have all built their nests in my beard!"

EDWARD LEAR

The New Colossus

Not like the brazen giant of Greek fame,
With conquering limbs astride from land to land;
Here at our sea-washed, sunset gates shall stand
A mighty woman with a torch, whose flame
Is the imprisoned lightning, and her name
Mother of Exiles. From her beacon-hand
Glows world-wide welcome; her mild eyes command
The air-bridged harbor, that twin cities frame.
"Keep, ancient lands, your storied pomp!" cries she
With silent lips. "Give me your tired, your poor,
Your huddled masses yearning to breathe free,
The wretched refuse of your teeming shore.
Send these, the homeless, tempest-tost to me,
I lift my lamp beside the golden door!"

EMMA LAZARUS

The Rough Little Rascal

A smudge on his nose and a smear on his cheek
And knees that might not have been washed in a week;
A bump on his forehead, a scar on his lip,
A relic of many a tumble and trip:
A rough little, tough little rascal, but sweet,
Is he that each evening I'm eager to meet.

A brow that is beady with jewels of sweat;
A face that's as black as a visage can get;
A suit that at noon was a garment of white,
Now one that his mother declares is a fright:
A fun-loving, sun-loving rascal, and fine,
Is he that comes placing his black fist in mine.

A crop of brown hair that is tousled and tossed;
A waist from which two of the buttons are lost;
A smile that shines out through the dirt and the grime,
And eyes that are flashing delight all the time:
All these are the joys that I'm eager to meet
And look for the moment I get to my street.

EDGAR A. GUEST

from *Song of Myself*

I am of old and young, of the foolish as much as the wise,
Regardless of others, ever regardful of others,
Maternal as well as paternal, a child as well as a man,
Stuff'd with the stuff that is coarse and stuff'd with the stuff
    that is fine,
One of the Nation of many nations, the smallest the same
    and the largest the same,
A Southerner soon as a Northerner, a planter nonchalant
    and hospitable down by the Oconee I live,
A Yankee bound my own way ready for trade, my joints the
    limberest joints on earth and the sternest joints on earth,
A Kentuckian walking the vale of the Elkhorn in my
    deer-skin leggings, a Louisianian or Georgian,
A boatman over lakes or bays or along coasts, a Hoosier,
    Badger, Buckeye;
At home on Kanadian snow-shoes or up in the bush, or
    with fishermen off Newfoundland,
At home in the fleet of ice-boats, sailing with the rest and
    tacking,
At home on the hills of Vermont or in the woods of Maine,
    or the Texan ranch,

Comrade of Californians, comrade of free North-Westerners,
    (loving their big proportions,)
Comrade of raftsmen and coalmen, comrade of all who
    shake hands and welcome to drink and meat,
A learner with the simplest, a teacher of the thoughtfullest,
A novice beginning yet experient of myriads of seasons,
Of every hue and caste am I, of every rank and religion,
A farmer, mechanic, artist, gentleman, sailor, quaker,
Prisoner, fancy-man, rowdy, lawyer, physician, priest.

I resist any thing better than my own diversity,
Breathe the air but leave plenty after me,
And am not stuck up, and am in my place.

WALT WHITMAN

maggie and milly and molly and may

maggie and milly and molly and may
went down to the beach (to play one day)

and maggie discovered a shell that sang
so sweetly she couldn't remember her troubles, and

milly befriended a stranded star
whose rays five languid fingers were;

and molly was chased by a horrible thing
which raced sideways while blowing bubbles: and

may came home with a smooth round stone
as small as a world and as large as alone.

For whatever we lose (like a you or a me)
it's always ourselves we find in the sea

E. E. CUMMINGS

Wasted Days

A fair slim boy not made for this world's pain.
With hair of gold thick clustering round his ears,
And longing eyes half veiled by foolish tears
Like bluest water seen through mists of rain:

Pale cheeks whereon no kiss hath left its stain,
Red under lip drawn for fear of Love,
And white throat whiter than the breast of dove.
Alas! alas! if all should be in vain.

Behind, wide fields, and reapers all a-row
In heat and labor toiling wearily,
To no sweet sound of laughter or of lute.
The sun is shooting wide its crimson glow,
Still the boy dreams: nor knows that night is nigh,
And in the night-time no man gathers fruit.

OSCAR WILDE

Which Are You?

There are two kinds of people on earth to-day;
Just two kinds of people, no more, I say.

Not the sinner and saint, for it's well understood,
The good are half bad, and the bad are half good.

Not the rich and the poor, for to rate a man's wealth,
You must first know the state of his conscience and health.

Not the humble and proud, for in life's little span,
Who puts on vain airs, is not counted a man.

Not the happy and sad, for the swift flying years
Bring each man his laughter and each man his tears.

No; the two kinds of people on earth I mean,
Are the people who lift, and the people who lean.

Wherever you go, you will find the earth's masses,
Are always divided in just these two classes.

And oddly enough, you will find too, I ween,
There's only one lifter to twenty who lean.

In which class are you? Are you easing the load,
Of overtaxed lifters, who toil down the road?

Or are you a leaner, who lets others share
Your portion of labor, and worry and care?

ELLA WHEELER WILCOX

Personal Reflection

Dream Variations

To fling my arms wide
In some place of the sun,
To whirl and to dance
Till the white day is done.
Then rest at cool evening
Beneath a tall tree
While night comes on gently,
    Dark like me—
That is my dream!

To fling my arms wide
In the face of the sun,
Dance! Whirl! Whirl!
Till the quick day is done.
Rest at pale evening . . .
A tall, slim tree . . .
Night coming tenderly
    Black like me.

LANGSTON HUGHES

Those Winter Sundays

Sundays too my father got up early
and put his clothes on in the blueback cold,
then with cracked hands that ached
from labor in the weekday weather made
banked fires blaze. No one ever thanked him.

I'd wake and hear the cold splintering, breaking.
When the rooms were warm, he'd call,
and slowly I would rise and dress,
fearing the chronic angers of that house,

Speaking indifferently to him,
who had driven out the cold
and polished my good shoes as well.
What did I know, what did I know
of love's austere and lonely offices?

ROBERT HAYDEN

Children

Come to me, O ye children!
For I hear you at your play,
And the questions that perplexed me
Have vanished quite away.

Ye open the eastern windows,
That look towards the sun,
Where thoughts are singing swallows
And the brooks of morning run.

In your hearts are the birds and the sunshine,
In your thoughts the brooklet's flow,
But in mine is the wind of Autumn
And the first fall of the snow.

Ah! what would the world be to us
If the children were no more?
We should dread the desert behind us
Worse than the dark before.

What the leaves are to the forest,
With light and air for food,
Ere their sweet and tender juices
Have been hardened into wood,—

That to the world are children;
Through them it feels the glow
Of a brighter and sunnier climate
Than reaches the trunks below.

Come to me, O ye children!
And whisper in my ear
What the birds and the winds are singing
In your sunny atmosphere.

For what are all our contrivings,
And the wisdom of our books,
When compared with your caresses,
And the gladness of your looks?

Ye are better than all the ballads
That ever were sung or said;
For ye are living poems,
And all the rest are dead.

HENRY WADSWORTH LONGFELLOW

The Waking

I wake to sleep, and take my waking slow.
I feel my fate in what I cannot fear.
I learn by going where I have to go.

We think by feeling. What is there to know?
I hear my being dance from ear to ear.
I wake to sleep, and take my waking slow.

Of those so close beside me, which are you?
God bless the Ground! I shall walk softly there,
And learn by going where I have to go.

Light takes the Tree; but who can tell us how?
The lowly worm climbs up a winding stair;
I wake to sleep, and take my waking slow.

Great Nature has another thing to do
To you and me; so take the lively air,
And, lovely, learn by going where to go.

This shaking keeps me steady. I should know.
What falls away is always. And is near.
I wake to sleep, and take my waking slow.
I learn by going where I have to go.

THEODORE ROETHKE

This is my letter to the world,

This is my letter to the world,
 That never wrote to me,—
The simple news that Nature told,
 With tender majesty.

Her message is committed
 To hands I cannot see;
For love of her, sweet countrymen,
 Judge tenderly of me!

EMILY DICKINSON

If—

If you can keep your head when all about you
    Are losing theirs and blaming it on you;
If you can trust yourself when all men doubt you,
    But make allowance for their doubting too;
If you can wait and not be tired by waiting,
    Or, being lied about, don't deal in lies,
Or, being hated, don't give way to hating,
    And yet don't look too good, nor talk too wise;

If you can dream—and not make dreams your master;
    If you can think—and not make thoughts your aim;
If you can meet with triumph and disaster
    And treat those two imposters just the same;
If you can bear to hear the truth you've spoken
    Twisted by knaves to make a trap for fools,
Or watch the things you gave your life to broken,
    And stoop and build 'em up with wornout tools;

If you can make one heap of all your winnings
    And risk it on one turn of pitch-and-toss,
And lose, and start again at your beginnings
    And never breathe a word about your loss;
If you can force your heart and nerve and sinew
    To serve your turn long after they are gone,
And so hold on when there is nothing in you
    Except the Will which says to them: "Hold on";

If you can talk with crowds and keep your virtue,
    Or walk with kings—nor lose the common touch;
If neither foes nor loving friends can hurt you;
    If all men count with you, but none too much;
If you can fill the unforgiving minute
With sixty seconds' worth of distance run—
    Yours is the Earth and everything that's in it,
And—which is more—you'll be a Man, my son!

RUDYARD KIPLING

Truthful words are not beautiful.

Truthful words are not beautiful.
Beautiful words are not truthful.
Good men do not argue.
Those who argue are not good.
Those who know are not learned.
The learned do not know.

The sage never tries to store things up.
The more he does for others, the more he has.
The more he gives to others, the greater his abundance.
The Tao of heaven is pointed but does no harm.
The Tao of the sage is work without effort.

LAO TZU

Choose

The single clenched fist lifted and ready,
Or the open asking hand held out and waiting.
   Choose:
For we meet by one or the other.

CARL SANDBURG

The Swing

How do you like to go up in a swing,
   Up in the air so blue?
Oh, I do think it the pleasantest thing
   Ever a child can do!

Up in the air and over the wall,
   Till I can see so wide,
Rivers and trees and cattle and all
   Over the countryside—

Till I look down on the garden green,
   Down on the roof so brown—
Up in the air I go flying again,
   Up in the air and down!

ROBERT LOUIS STEVENSON

On the Beach at Night Alone

On the beach at night alone,
As the old mother sways her to and fro singing her husky song,
As I watch the bright stars shining, I think a thought of the clef
    of the universes and of the future.

A vast similitude interlocks all,
All spheres, grown, ungrown, small, large, suns, moons, planets;
All distances of place however wide,
All distances of time, all inanimate forms,
All souls, all living bodies though they be ever so different,
    or in different worlds,
All gaseous, watery, vegetable, mineral processes, the fishes,
    the brutes,
All nations, colors, barbarisms, civilizations, languages,
All identities that have existed or may exist on this globe, or
    any globe,
All lives and deaths, all of the past, present, future,
This vast similitude spans them, and always has spann'd,
And shall forever span them and compactly hold and
    enclose them.

WALT WHITMAN

Life

Life, believe, is not a dream
   So dark as sages say;
Oft a little morning rain
   Foretells a pleasant day.
Sometimes there are clouds of gloom,
   But these are transient all;
If the shower will make the roses bloom,
   O why lament its fall?

   Rapidly, merrily,
Life's sunny hours flit by,
   Gratefully, cheerily,
Enjoy them as they fly!

What though Death at times steps in
   And calls our Best away?
What though sorrow seems to win,
   O'er hope, a heavy sway?
Yet hope again elastic springs,
   Unconquered, though she fell;
Still buoyant are her golden wings,
   Still strong to bear us well.
   Manfully, fearlessly,
The day of trial bear,
   For gloriously, victoriously,
Can courage quell despair!

CHARLOTTE BRONTË

If I can stop one heart from breaking,

If I can stop one heart from breaking,
I shall not live in vain;
If I can ease one life the aching,
Or cool one pain,
Or help one fainting robin
Unto his nest again,
I shall not live in vain.

EMILY DICKINSON

from Book 1 of *Endymion*

A thing of beauty is a joy for ever:
Its loveliness increases; it will never
Pass into nothingness; but still will keep
A bower quiet for us, and a sleep
Full of sweet dreams, and health, and quiet breathing.

JOHN KEATS

*My house says to me, "Do not leave me, for
here dwells your past."*

My house says to me, "Do not leave me, for here dwells your
past."
And the road says to me, "Come and follow me, for I am
your future."
And I say to both my house and the road, "I have no past,
nor have I a future. If I stay here, there is a going in my
staying; and if I go there is a staying in my going. Only
love and death will change all things."

KAHLIL GIBRAN

I never saw a moor,

I never saw a moor,
I never saw the sea;
Yet know I how the heather looks,
And what a wave must be.

I never spoke with God,
Nor visited in heaven;
Yet certain am I of the spot
As if the chart were given.

EMILY DICKINSON

A Patriotic Wish

I'd like to be the sort of man the flag could boast about;
I'd like to be the sort of man it cannot live without;
I'd like to be the type of man
That really is American:
The head-erect and shoulders-square,
Clean-minded fellow, just and fair,
That all men picture when they see
The glorious banner of the free.

I'd like to be the sort of man the flag now typifies,
The kind of man we really want the flag to symbolize;
The loyal brother to a trust,
The big, unselfish soul and just,
The friend of every man oppressed,
The strong support of all that's best,
The sturdy chap the banner's meant,
Where'er it flies, to represent.

I'd like to be the sort of man the flag's supposed to mean,
The man that all in fancy see wherever it is seen,
The chap that's ready for a fight
Whenever there's a wrong to right,
The friend in every time of need,
The doer of the daring deed,
The clean and generous handed man
That is a real American.

EDGAR A. GUEST

A Book.

He ate and drank the precious words,
His spirit grew robust;
He knew no more that he was poor,
Nor that his frame was dust.
He danced along the dingy days,
And this bequest of wings
Was but a book. What liberty
A loosened spirit brings!

EMILY DICKINSON

Great Friend

I walk in nature still alone
And know no one
Discern no lineament nor feature
Of any creature.

Though all the firmament
Is o'er me bent,
Yet still I miss the grace
Of an intelligent and kindred face.

I still must seek the friend
Who does with nature blend,
Who is the person in her mask,
He is the man I ask.

Who is the expression of her meaning,
Who is the uprightness of her leaning,
Who is the grown child of her weaning.

The center of this world,
The face of nature,
The site of human life,
Some sure foundation
And nucleus of a nation—
At least a private station.

We twain would walk together
Through every weather,
And see this aged nature,
Go with a bending stature.

HENRY DAVID THOREAU

The Power of Words

'Tis a strange mystery, the power of words!
Life is in them, and death. A word can send
The crimson color hurrying to the cheek.
Hurrying with many meanings; or can turn
The current cold and deadly to the heart.
Anger and fear are in them; grief and joy
Are on their sound; yet slight, impalpable:—
A word is but a breath of passing air.

L.E.L. (LETITIA ELIZABETH LANDON)

Selfish

I am selfish in my wishin' every sort o' joy for you;
I am selfish when I tell you that I'm wishin' skies o' blue
Bending o'er you every minute, and a pocketful of gold,
An' as much of love an' gladness as a human heart can hold.
Coz I know beyond all question that if such a thing could be
As you cornerin' life's riches you would share 'em all with me.

I am selfish in my wishin' every sorrow from your way,
With no trouble thoughts to fret you at the closin' o' the day;
An' it's selfishness that bids me wish you comforts by the score,
An' all the joys you long for, an' on top o' them, some more;
Coz I know, old tried an' faithful, that if such a thing could be
As you cornerin' life's riches you would share 'em all with me.

EDGAR A. GUEST

My Shadow

I have a little shadow that goes in and out with me,
And what can be the use of him is more than I can see.
He is very, very like me from the heels up to the head;
And I see him jump before me, when I jump into my bed.

The funniest thing about him is the way he likes to grow—
Not at all like proper children, which is always very slow;
For he sometimes shoots up taller like an India-rubber ball,
And he sometimes gets so little that there's none of him at all.

He hasn't got a notion of how children ought to play,
And can only make a fool of me in every sort of way.
He stays so close beside me, he's a coward you can see;
I'd think shame to stick to nursie as that shadow sticks to me!

One morning, very early, before the sun was up,
I rose and found the shining dew on every buttercup;
But my lazy little shadow, like an arrant sleepy-head,
Had stayed at home behind me and was fast asleep in bed.

ROBERT LOUIS STEVENSON

Failures

'Tis better to have tried in vain,
   Sincerely striving for a goal,
Than to have lived upon the plain
   An idle and a timid soul.

'Tis better to have fought and spent
   Your courage, missing all applause,
Than to have lived in smug content
   And never ventured for a cause.

For he who tries and fails may be
   The founder of a better day;
Though never his the victory,
   From him shall others learn the way.

EDGAR A. GUEST

Farewells

Remember

Remember me when I am gone away,
Gone far away into the silent land;
When you can no more hold me by the hand,
Nor I half turn to go, yet turning stay.
Remember me when no more, day by day,
You tell me of our future that you planned;
Only remember me; you understand
It will be late to counsel then or pray.
Yet if you should forget me for a while
And afterwards remember, do not grieve;
For if the darkness and corruption leave
A vestige of the thoughts that once I had,
Better by far you should forget and smile
Than that you should remember and be sad.

CHRISTINA GEORGINA ROSSETTI

Streets

A man leaves the world
and the streets he lived on
grow a little shorter.

One more window dark
in this city, the figs on his branches
will soften for birds.

If we stand quietly enough evenings
there grows a whole company of us
standing quietly together.
Overhead loud grackles are claiming their trees
and the sky which sews and sews, tirelessly sewing,
drops her purple hem.
Each thing in its time, in its place,
it would be nice to think the same about people.

Some people do. They sleep completely,
waking refreshed. Others live in two worlds,
the lost and remembered.
They sleep twice, once for the one who is gone,
once for themselves. They dream thickly,
dream double, they wake from a dream
into another one, they walk the short streets
calling out names, and then they answer.

NAOMI SHIHAB NYE

Annabel Lee

It was many and many a year ago,
   In a kingdom by the sea,
That a maiden there lived whom you may know
   By the name of Annabel Lee;
And this maiden she lived with no other thought
   Than to love and be loved by me.

I was a child and she was a child,
   In this kingdom by the sea,
But we loved with a love that was more than love,
   I and my Annabel Lee;
With a love that the wingèd seraphs of heaven
   Coveted her and me.

And this was the reason that, long ago,
   In this kingdom by the sea,
A wind blew out of a cloud, chilling
   My beautiful Annabel Lee;
So that her highborn kinsmen came
   And bore her away from me,
To shut her up in a sepulchre
   In this kingdom by the sea.

The angels, not half so happy in heaven,
   Went envying her and me,
Yes! that was the reason (as all men know,
   In this kingdom by the sea)
That the wind came out of the cloud by night,
   Chilling and killing my Annabel Lee.

But our love it was stronger by far than the love
   Of those who were older than we,
   Of many far wiser than we;
And neither the angels in heaven above,
   Nor the demons down under the sea,
Can ever dissever my soul from the soul
   Of the beautiful Annabel Lee:

For the moon never beams, without bringing me dreams
   Of the beautiful Annabel Lee;
And the stars never rise, but I feel the bright eyes
   Of the beautiful Annabel Lee;
And so, all the night-tide, I lie down by the side
Of my darling—my darling—my life and my bride,
   In her sepulchre there by the sea,
   In her tomb by the sounding sea.

EDGAR ALLAN POE

Farewell to the Farm

The coach is at the door at last;
The eager children, mounting fast
And kissing hands, in chorus sing:
Good-bye, good-bye, to everything!

To house and garden, field and lawn,
The meadow-gates we swang upon,
To pump and stable, tree and swing,
Good-bye, good-bye, to everything!

And fare you well for evermore,
O ladder at the hayloft door,
O hayloft where the cobwebs cling,
Good-bye, good-bye, to everything!

Crack goes the whip, and off we go;
The trees and houses smaller grow;
Last, round the woody turn we sing:
Good-bye, good-bye, to everything!

ROBERT LOUIS STEVENSON

Parting

As from our dream we died away
Far off I felt the outer things;
Your wind-blown tresses round me play,
Your bosom's gentle murmurings.

And far away our faces met
As on the verge of the vast spheres;
And in the night our cheeks were wet,
I could not say with dew or tears.

O gate by which I entered in!
O face and hair! O lips and eyes!
Through you again the world I win,
How far away from Paradise!

GEORGE WILLIAM RUSSELL ("A.E.")

Recollection

How can it be that I forget
     The way he phrased my doom,
When I recall the arabesques
     That carpeted the room?

How can it be that I forget
     His look and mein that hour,
When I recall I wore a rose,
     And still can smell the flower?

How can it be that I forget
     Those words that were his last,
When I recall the tune a man
     Was whistling as he passed?

These things are what we keep from life's
     Supremest joy or pain;
For memory locks her chaff in bins
     And throws away the grain.

ANNE REEVE ALDRICH

The Hills of Rest

Beyond the last horizon's rim
    Beyond adventure's farthest quest,
Somewhere they rise, serene and dim,
    The happy, happy Hills of Rest.

Upon their sunlit slopes uplift
    The castles we have built in Spain—
While fair amid the summer drift
    Our faded gardens flower again.

Sweet hours we did not live go by
    To soothing note, on scented wing;
In golden-lettered volumes lie
    The songs we tried in vain to sing.

They are all there, the days of dream
    That build the inner lives of men;
The silent, sacred years we deem
    The might be and the might have been.

Some evening when the sky is gold
    I'll follow day into the west;
Nor pause, nor heed, till I behold
    The happy, happy Hills of Rest.

ALBERT BIGELOW PAINE

Index of Poets

Index to First Lines

(Acknowledgments continued from page 2.)

LANGSTON HUGHES: "City," "Dream Variations," and "April Rain Song." From THE COLLECTED POEMS OF LANGSTON HUGHES by Langston Hughes, copyright © 1994 by The Estate of Langston Hughes. Used by permission of Alfred A. Knopf, a division of Random House, Inc.

JAMES JOYCE: "Winds of May, that dance on the sea,". Originally published in CHAMBER MUSIC by James Joyce (London: E. Mathews, 1907).

NAOMI SHIHAB NYE: "Streets" from WORDS UNDER THE WORDS: Selected Poems by Naomi Shihab Nye. Copyright © 1995 by Naomi Shihab Nye. Published by Far Corner Books.

THEODORE ROETHKE: "The Waking," copyright © 1953 by Theodore Roethke, from THE COLLECTED POEMS OF THEODORE ROETHKE. Used by permission of Doubleday, a division of Random House, Inc.

CARL SANDBURG: "Daybreak" from WIND SONG, copyright © 1958 by Carl Sandburg and renewed 1986 by Margaret Sandburg, Janet Sandburg, and Helga Sandburg Crile, reprinted by permission of Harcourt, Inc. "Fog" and "Choose." Originally published in CHICAGO POEMS by Carl Sandburg (New York: Henry Holt & Co., 1916).

WILLIAM CARLOS WILLIAMS: "Winter Trees" by William Carlos Williams, from COLLECTED POEMS: 1909-1939, VOLUME I, copyright © 1938 by New Directions Publishing Corp. Reprinted by permission of New Directions Publishing Corp.

WILLIAM BUTLER YEATS: "The Poet pleads with his Friend for old Friends." Originally published in THE WIND AMONG THE REEDS by W. B. Yeats (New York: J. Lane, 1899). "When You Are Old." Originally published in THE ROSE (1893).